WeeSing® & Learn
MY BODY

Library of Congress Cataloging-in-Publication Data

Beall, Pamela Conn.
 Wee sing & learn my body / by Pamela Conn Beall and Susan Hagen Nipp;
illustrated by Winky Adam.
     p. cm.
Summary: Shows children various body parts, from head to toe, inviting
the reader to show what they can do with their own bodies.
 1. Body, Human—Juvenile literature. [1. Body, Human.] I. Title: Wee
sing and learn my body. II. Nipp, Susan Hagen. III. Adam, Winky, ill.
IV. Title.
 QM27 .B426 2003
 611—dc21
                                                        2002151542

            ISBN 0-8341-0255-1   A B C D E F G H I J

     PSS! and Wee Sing are registered trademarks of Penguin Group (USA) Inc.

Wee Sing® & Learn
MY BODY

by Pamela Conn Beall and Susan Hagen Nipp
illustrated by Winky Adam

PSS!
PRICE STERN SLOAN

my body

My body can do lots of things.

head

This is my head.

What can you do with your head?

eyes

These are my eyes.

What can you do with your eyes?

nose

This is my nose.

What can you do with your nose?

mouth

This is my mouth.

What can you do with your mouth?

ears

These are my ears.

What can you do with your ears?

arms

These are my arms.

What can you do with your arms?

hands

These are my hands.

What can you do with your hands?

fingers

These are my fingers.

What can you do with your fingers?

legs

These are my legs.

What can you do with your legs?

knees

These are my knees.

What can you do with your knees?

feet

These are my feet.

What can you do with your feet?

toes

These are my toes.

What can you do with your toes?

How are these children using their bodies?

Point to your own body parts.

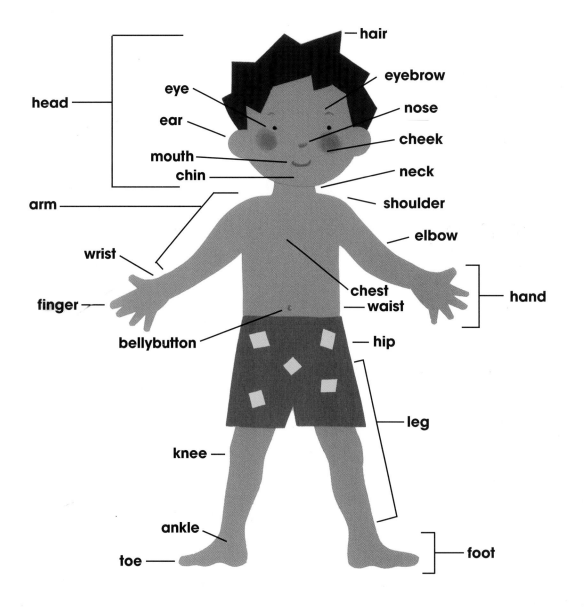

hair

eyebrow

nose

cheek

eye

ear

mouth

chin

neck

shoulder

head

arm

elbow

wrist

chest

finger

waist

hand

bellybutton

hip

leg

knee

ankle

toe

foot